J.R. Lofthouse.

Praying with the Bible

Praying
with the Bible

Compiled by

PHILIP LAW

First published in Great Britain in 2007

Society for Promoting Christian Knowledge
36 Causton Street
London SW1P 4ST

British Library Cataloguing-in-Publication Data
A catalogue record for this book is available from the British Library

ISBN 978–0–281–05917–1

1 3 5 7 9 10 8 6 4 2

Produced on paper from sustainable forests

Typeset by Kenneth Burnley, Wirral, Cheshire
Printed in Great Britain by CPI Antony Rowe Ltd

Contents

An asterisk (*) following the Bible reference after a prayer indicates that the Bible text has been adapted or expanded.

Introduction

Prayer is an essential part of the Christian life. Through prayer we can draw near to God and God can draw near to us; through prayer we can increase and enrich our love for others; and through prayer we can find the peace of God that transcends all understanding (James 4.8; 1 Thessalonians 3.12; Philippians 4.7).

Five Facets of Prayer

To what can we liken prayer? It is like a precious jewel, with five facets reflecting the light of human love for God, who is the origin and the object of all prayer. These five facets, or forms, of prayer are all found in the Bible, and all are represented in this anthology.

1. Adoration: Trusting in God's Goodness

Some of the most encouraging words ever written on prayer are to be found in this passage from the New Testament:

> Therefore since we have a great high priest who has gone through the heavens, Jesus, the Son of God, let us hold firmly to the faith we profess. For we do not have a high priest who is unable to sympathise with our weaknesses, but we have one who has been tempted in every way, just as we are – yet was without sin. Let us then approach the throne of grace with confidence, so that we may receive mercy and find grace to help us in our time of need.
>
> (Hebrews 4.14–16)

Because he lived as one of us, because he felt the same joys and sorrows, and because he was tempted by sin just as we are, Jesus feels a deep sympathy with everyone who prays, as he did, for God's help. Because he feels this sympathy, Jesus is now the perfect mediator between God and humanity. And because we have this perfect mediator, we can pray to God with confidence, trusting completely in the grace and goodness only God can give.

We can have such confidence because, in the words of the apostle Paul:

> The Spirit helps us in our weakness; for we do not know how to pray as we ought, but that very Spirit intercedes with sighs too deep for words. And God, who searches the heart, knows what is the mind of the Spirit, because the Spirit intercedes for the saints according to the will of God.
> (Romans 8.26–27)

These words help us to understand how Jesus acts as our mediator. It is by the all-pervading power of the Holy Spirit that the Son presents our prayers to God the Father. And because of this, no matter how weak and inarticulate our prayers may be, no matter how unworthy or sinful we may feel, we can be confident that God will hear and understand.

On a human level, we place our confidence in the people we know and love the most. It is our closest relatives and friends to whom we turn for help in times of need, and in whom we confide our inmost thoughts and feelings. They are the ones we trust.

And so it is with prayer. Through Jesus, we can confide in God. Everything that matters to us, whether big or small, good or bad, whatever we need to talk about and find answers to, we can entrust to God in prayer.

Trusting God in this way infuses into our prayers a feeling of love and adoration for the One who, through Jesus, makes it possible for us to live our lives in ways that reflect God's goodness. As the apostle John explains:

God is love, and whoever lives in love lives in union with God and God lives in union with him. Love is made perfect in us in order that we may have courage ... There is no fear in love; perfect love drives out fear.

(1 John 4.16–18)

And so it is that the prayer of adoration is above all the prayer of fearless trust in the goodness of God, enabling us to draw near, receive mercy and find grace to help in time of need.

2. Confession: Seeking God's Forgiveness

Confiding in another person is bound to involve, at some point, the act of confession. Something we have said or done is on our conscience and we need to unburden it to someone: to admit it, face up to it, seek forgiveness for it, and, if possible, put it right.

When we come to confide in God, it is vital that we first confess our sins. For sin is the barrier we are constantly trying to overcome in the very act of praying, and if we do not first confront our sin, confess it and truly repent of it, we may find that we are praying to ourselves and not to God.

This is what Jesus was warning against when he told the story about two very different men who went up to the Temple to pray:

He spoke the following parable to some people who prided themselves on being upright and despised everyone else. 'Two men went up to the Temple to pray, one a Pharisee, the other a tax collector. The Pharisee stood there and said this prayer to himself, "I thank you, God, that I am not grasping, unjust, adulterous like everyone else, and particularly that I am not like this tax collector here. I fast twice a week; I pay tithes on all I get." The tax collector stood some distance away, not daring even to raise his eyes to heaven; but he beat on his breast and said, "God, be merciful to me, a sinner." This man, I tell you, went home again justified; the other did not. For everyone who raises himself up will be humbled, and anyone who humbles himself will be raised up.'

(Luke 18.9–14)

The problem with the Pharisee was that his confidence was misplaced. He had reached a point where he was trusting in himself rather than God, and this self-confidence had hardened into a form of self-righteous pride that was really nothing short of self-delusion.

John's First Letter makes it clear:

> If we say that we have no sin, we deceive ourselves, and there is no truth in us. But if we confess our sins to God, he will . . . forgive our sins and purify us from all our wrong-doing.

(1 John 1.8–9)

The aim of the prayer of confession, then, is to cleanse us from sin and purify our hearts in God's presence. And this we need to do whenever we approach God in prayer.

> Be merciful to me, O God,
> because of your constant love.
> Wash away all my evil
> and make me clean from my sin!
> Create a pure heart in me, O God,
> and put a new and loyal spirit in me.
> (Psalm 51.1, 2, 10)

3. Thanksgiving: Praising God's Greatness

Thanksgiving – for all that God is, and all that God has done – is a facet of prayer reflected in every part of the Bible; no more so than in the life and words of Jesus:

> I thank you, Father, Lord of heaven and earth, because you have hidden these things from the wise and the intelligent

and have revealed them to infants; yes, Father, for such was
your gracious will.

(Matthew 11.25–26)

The word translated here as 'thank' is the same as the word used
elsewhere in the New Testament for 'confess', suggesting to us
the importance of acknowledging our blessings as well as our
sins. Too much time dwelling on our sins may lead to an
unhealthy, morbid and depressing prayer life, which is why Paul
encouraged the early believers to 'always be joyful; pray constantly; and for all things give thanks' (1 Thessalonians 5.16–18).

Paul's letters often opened with outbursts of thanksgiving:

Let us give thanks to the God and Father of our Lord Jesus
Christ, the merciful Father, the God from whom all help
comes!

(2 Corinthians 1.3)

We always give thanks to God, the Father of our Lord Jesus
Christ, when we pray for you.

(Colossians 1.3)

In these letters, the prayer of thanksgiving is interchangeable
with the prayer of praise:

Let us give thanks to the God and Father of our Lord Jesus
Christ! For in our union with Christ he has blessed us . . .

Let us praise God for his glorious grace, for the free gift he
has given us in his dear Son!

(Ephesians 1.3, 6)

The same is true of the many prayers of thanksgiving and praise
in the book of Psalms:

Praise the Lord, because he is good; sing praises to his name, because he is kind.

(Psalm 135.3)

Give thanks to the Lord, because he is good; his love is eternal.

(Psalm 136.1)

Genuine, heartfelt gratitude for God's greatness and goodness is an essential facet of Christian life as well as Christian prayer. If we are thankful for God's love, we will be loving to others; if we are thankful for God's justice, we will be just to others; if we are thankful for God's grace, we will be gracious to others. As Paul said:

Whatever you do, in word or deed, do everything in the name of the Lord Jesus, giving thanks to God the Father through him.

(Colossians 3.17)

4. Petition: Asking God's Help

Much of prayer involves asking God for what we need, but Paul reminds us that any asking we do should be accompanied with thanksgiving:

Don't worry about anything, but in all your prayers ask God for what you need, always asking him with a thankful heart.

(Philippians 4.6)

In other words, although God is gracious, God will not be taken for granted. God wants to grant our prayers of petition, but first God wants us to be truly grateful for all the blessings we already enjoy.

Note also that Paul says that in all our prayers we should ask God for what we *need*, not what we *want*. The two may not necessarily be the same! And this means that our prayers of petition have to incorporate a willingness to accept that some of our petitions may not accord with God's will, and may not therefore be fulfilled. In the words of John's First Letter:

> We have courage in God's presence, because we are sure that he hears us if we ask for anything that is according to his will.
>
> (1 John 5.14)

Think of the prayer that Jesus prayed as he faced the prospect of crucifixion:

> 'Father,' he prayed, 'my Father! All things are possible for you. Take this cup of suffering away from me. Yet not what I want, but what you want.'
>
> (Mark 14.36)

In one sense, this prayer of Jesus was refused: God did not take away the cup of suffering. But that does not mean that Jesus' prayer was not heard. On the contrary, God heard and answered this prayer by giving Jesus the strength he needed to endure the sufferings that awaited him, and by raising him from death when those sufferings were over.

> In the course of his earthly life he offered up prayers and petitions, with loud cries and tears, to God who was able to deliver him from death. Because of his devotion his prayer was heard: son though he was, he learned obedience through his sufferings.
>
> (Hebrews 5.7–8)

The writer here draws attention to something else we need to remember when we pray the prayer of petition. If we want our petitions to be answered, we must learn not only to *pray* but also to *live* in accord with God's will. In other words, like Jesus, we need to learn obedience.

For example, we may petition God each day for strength to overcome a particular fault or temptation. But what kind of prayer is this if, after praying, we make little or no effort to overcome that fault or resist that temptation? For prayers of petition to be worth praying at all, God wants us to have at least the *will* to obey, and the determination to do what God finds pleasing.

> If our conscience does not condemn us, we have courage in God's presence. We receive from him whatever we ask, because we obey his commands and do what pleases him.
>
> (1 John 3.21, 22)

5. Intercession: Loving God's World

So far, the facets of prayer we have thought about – adoration, confession, thanksgiving and petition – have all been to do with the relationship that prayer creates between God and ourselves. With the fifth and final facet, we come to the relationship between God, ourselves and the world around us.

Here again, Jesus has left the supreme example. His prayers of intercession for others extended even to his enemies. Even as they tortured him to death, he prayed, 'Father, forgive them; for they know not what they do' (Luke 23.34).

Our prayers must also extend to those with whom, at any time and for whatever reason, we may be at enmity. 'Love your enemies,' said Jesus, 'pray for those who treat you badly' (Luke 6.27, 28). But while our intercessions should never exclude our enemies, normally they will involve prayers for people we regard as friends – or who at least have done us no harm.

Such prayers of intercession will often arise as a result of someone we know being in special need of help and support through a time of crisis. And here again, as with the prayer of petition, the prayer of intercession needs to be lived as well as prayed. 'Our love', wrote John, 'should not be just words and talk; it must be true love, showing itself in action' (1 John 3.18).

Unlike those who lived in biblical times, we are aware today of many more needs and concerns in the world beyond those of our immediate family, friends or locality. But the principle of intercession remains the same. We pray for people in other parts of the world to be relieved of their suffering – whether from war, oppression, economic deprivation or natural disaster; we pray for the end of human greed and conflict; we pray for those in power to make wise decisions about the earth's future and its resources. But all the time, we need to remember to live as well as to pray these intercessions. Depending on our circumstances, there may not be much that we can do; but, however little it may be, even if no more than a small donation to a relief effort, our prayers will surely count for more if we are loving and caring for God's world by giving back to it something of our own.

Praying with the Bible

In all these facets of prayer, Jesus provides the ultimate example of how to pray with integrity. For his prayers and his actions were so perfectly integrated that the whole of his life became a prayer to God. Prayer – in other words, communion with God – became his life; for no other person has lived, as Jesus lived, in complete, unbroken awareness of God's presence, and in complete, unbroken obedience to God's will.

Jesus often used the Scriptures when he prayed. He resisted temptation in the wilderness, saying, 'Scripture says, "Worship the Lord your God and serve only him"' (Luke 4.8). On the cross he cried out in the words of Psalm 22, 'My God, my God, why have you abandoned me?' (Matthew 27.46). By following Jesus' example, we too can allow God's word to enter our hearts, and to permeate all our thoughts and actions.

When we pray with the Bible we can be encouraged in the knowledge that we are praying in a long line of Christian tradition that dates back through the centuries to Jesus himself. We can also be encouraged by the thought that Christians throughout the world, and in many languages, are voicing these same prayers to our heavenly Father.

Praying with the Bible in this way helps to give our daily prayer-life focus and structure. It helps to prevent our prayers from becoming like those of the Pharisee in the Temple – self-involved and self-indulgent. It can also help us in particular times of crisis. Here, the short 'arrow' prayers that appear in this anthology can be especially useful. We may find ourselves praying, like Jesus, 'Father, into your hands I commend my spirit' (Luke 23.46); or, like Peter, 'Lord, save me!' (Matthew 14.30); or, like the prodigal son, 'Father, I have sinned against heaven, and before you' (Luke 15.18).

Prayers such as these can also be used at times when we struggle to find the right words: when we are distraught, angry or even overcome with joy. The Bible includes prayers expressing the whole range of human emotions.

The final part of this anthology, 'Contemplation: Listening to God's Words', comprises short biblical phrases, intended for those who would like to include a contemplative element in their prayers. The phrases from the Old Testament (pages 118–25) are those in which God speaks directly to his people – strengthening, warning and forgiving them. The phrases from the New Testament (pages 126–30) are those in which Jesus, the incarnate Word of God, communicates God's inexhaustible love to all who will stop, become still and listen.

The practice of focusing attention each day on just one or two of these phrases – either from the Old Testament or from the Gospels – can lead you to a deepening awareness of God's presence, and give you that inner peace and spiritual confidence that only God can give.

I pray that the prayers collected here will help you to follow the example of Jesus in the way he prayed, drawing on the deep well of Scripture, and living in deeper harmony with the One whom he taught us to call 'Our Father'.

April 2007

Our Father in heaven:
May your holy name be honoured;
may your Kingdom come;
may your will be done on earth as it is in heaven.
Give us today the food we need.
Forgive us the wrongs we have done,
as we forgive the wrongs that others have done to us.
Do not bring us to hard testing,
but keep us safe from the Evil One.

Matthew 6.9–13

PART 1

ADORATION

TRUSTING IN GOD'S GOODNESS

Longing for God

As a deer longs for a stream of cool water,
so I long for you, O God.
I thirst for you, the living God;
when can I go and worship in your presence?
Day and night I cry,
and tears are my only food.
Why am I so sad?
Why am I so troubled?
I will put my hope in God,
and once again I will praise him,
my saviour and my God.

Psalm 42.1–3, 5

Lord of heaven and earth,
you made the world and everything in it;
you give life and breath to all things.
We seek you, yet you are not far from every one of us:
for in you we live, and move, and have our being.

Acts 17.24–28*

GOD WHO SEES

Why does the way of the guilty prosper?
Why do all who are treacherous thrive?
You plant them, and they take root;
they grow and bring forth fruit;
you are near in their mouths yet far from their hearts.
But you, O Lord, know me;
you see me and test me – my heart is with you.

Jeremiah 12.1–3

Lord, you made the heavens and the earth
by your great power and outstretched arm.
To you nothing is impossible.
Great and mighty God,
great in purpose, mighty in deed,
whose eyes are open to all human ways,
rewarding every person as they deserve!

Jeremiah 32.17–18*

There is hope

Speak first, O God, and I will answer.
Or let me speak, and you answer me.
What are my sins?
What wrongs have I done?
What crimes am I charged with?
Why do you avoid me?
Why do you treat me like an enemy?
Are you trying to frighten me?
I'm nothing but a leaf;
you are attacking a piece of dry straw.
You bring bitter charges against me,
even for what I did when I was young.
You bind chains on my feet;
you watch every step I take,
and even examine my footprints.
As a result, I crumble like rotten wood,
like a moth-eaten coat.

We are all born weak and helpless.
All lead the same short, troubled life.
We grow and wither as quickly as flowers;
we disappear like shadows.
There is hope for a tree that has been cut down;
it can come back to life and sprout.
Even though its roots grow old,
and its stump dies in the ground,
with water it will sprout like a young plant.
But people die, and that is the end of them;
they die, and where are they then?

Like rivers that stop running, and lakes that go dry,
people die, never to rise.
They will never wake up while the sky endures;
they will never stir from their sleep.

But I will wait for better times,
wait till this time of trouble is ended.
Then you will call, and I will answer,
and you will be pleased with me, your creature.
Then you will watch every step I take,
but you will not keep track of my sins.
You will forgive them and put them away;
you will wipe out all the wrongs I have done.

Job 13.22–28; 14.1–2, 7–12, 14–17

YOU HEARD MY PLEA

I called on your name, O Lord,
from the depths of the pit;
you heard my plea,
'Do not close your ear to my cry for help,
but give me relief!'
You came near when I called on you;
you said, 'Do not fear!'
You have taken up my cause, O Lord,
you have redeemed my life.

Lamentations 3.55–58

GOD ALONE

You are Lord alone;
you have made heaven, the heaven of heavens,
with all their host,
the earth and seas, and everything in them,
and you preserve them all;
and the host of heaven worships you.

Now therefore, our God,
the great, the mighty, and the terrible God,
who keeps covenant and mercy,
let not our troubles seem little before you.

Nehemiah 9.6, 32*

O Lord my God, you alone will I worship.
Nothing else in heaven or earth can take your place.

Deuteronomy 5.6–8*

ALL I HAVE

You, Lord, are all I have,
and you give me all I need;
my future is in your hands.
How wonderful are your gifts to me;
how good they are!

I praise the Lord, because he guides me,
and in the night my conscience warns me.
I am always aware of the Lord's presence;
he is near, and nothing can shake me.

And so I am thankful and glad,
and I feel completely secure,
because you protect me from the power of death,
and the one you love you will not
abandon to the world of the dead.

You will show me the path that leads to life;
your presence fills me with joy
and brings me pleasure for ever.

Psalm 16.5–11

IN YOU, O LORD, WE TRUST

Your love, O Lord, reaches the heavens,
your faithfulness extends to the skies.

In you, O Lord, we trust.

Your righteousness is like the mighty mountains,
your justice is like the great deep.

In you, O Lord, we trust.

How priceless is your unfailing love!
We find refuge in the shadow of your wings.

In you, O Lord, we trust.

For with you is the fountain of life;
in your light we see light.

In you, O Lord, we trust.

Psalm 36.5–9*

O GOD, YOU ARE MY GOD

O God, you are my God,
earnestly I seek you.

O God, you are my God.

My soul thirsts for you, my body longs for you,
in a dry and weary land where there is no water.

O God, you are my God.

I have seen you in the sanctuary
and beheld your power and your glory.

O God, you are my God.

Because your love is better than life,
my lips will glorify you.

O God, you are my God.

I will praise you as long as I live,
and in your name I will lift up my hands.

O God, you are my God.

Because you are my help,
I sing in the shadow of your wings.

O God, you are my God.

Psalm 63.1–7*

We bow our heads before you

Lord, you have been our dwelling-place
in all generations.
Before the mountains were brought forth,
or ever you had formed the earth and the world,
from everlasting to everlasting you are God.

We bow our heads before you.

You turn us back to dust, and say,
'Turn back, you mortals.'
For a thousand years in your sight
are like yesterday when it is past,
or like a watch in the night.

We bow our heads before you.

You sweep them away; they are like a dream,
like grass that is renewed in the morning;
in the morning it flourishes and is renewed;
in the evening it fades and withers.

We bow our heads before you.

For all our days pass away under your wrath;
our years come to an end like a sigh.
The days of our life are seventy years,
or perhaps eighty, if we are strong;
even then their span is only toil and trouble;
they are soon gone, and we fly away.

We bow our heads before you.

Psalm 90.1–10*

GREAT IS YOUR LOVE

Lord of compassion,
gracious, long-suffering and ever faithful,
you will not always accuse,
or nurse your anger for ever;
you have not treated us as our sins deserve
or repaid us according to our misdeeds.
As the heavens tower high above the earth,
so outstanding is your love towards those who fear you.
As far as the east is from the west,
so far have you put away our offences.
As a father has compassion on his children,
so you have compassion on those who fear you.
For you know, O Lord, how we were made;
you remember that we are but dust.

Psalm 103.8–14*

Your love, O God, is as strong as death;
your ardour unyielding as the grave.
It burns like a blazing fire, like a mighty flame.
Many waters cannot quench it;
rivers cannot wash it away.

Song of Songs 8.6–7*

GOD OF LOVE

Father, you have taught us to love one another,
because love is from you;
everyone who loves is born of you and knows you.
Whoever does not love does not know you, for you are love.

God of love, we love you.

You revealed your love among us
by sending your only Son into the world
so that we might live through him.

God of love, we love you.

In this is love, not that we loved you
but that you loved us and sent your Son
to be the atoning sacrifice for our sins.

God of love, we love you.

Since you loved us so much,
we also ought to love one another.
If we love one another, you live in us,
and your love is perfected in us.

God of love, we love you.

By this we know that we abide in you and you in us,
because you have given us of your Spirit.
And you have sent your Son as the Saviour of the world.

God of love, we love you.

1 John 4.7–14*

GOD OF STRENGTH

God, give me strength and good courage;
let me not be afraid,
neither let me be dismayed:
for I know you are with me wherever I go.

Joshua 1.9*

Lord, you are the one who protects me
and gives me strength;
you help me in times of trouble.

Jeremiah 16.19

GOD OF PEACE

Lord, I have given up my pride
and turned away from my arrogance.
I am not concerned with great matters
or with subjects too difficult for me.
Instead, I am content and at peace.
As a child lies quietly in its mother's arms,
so my heart is quiet within me.

Psalm 131.1–2

You, Lord, give perfect peace
to those who keep their purpose firm
and put their trust in you.
We follow your will and put our hope in you;
you are all that we desire.

Isaiah 26.3, 8

GOD OF COMFORT

O Lord, I will praise you:
though you were angry with me,
your anger is turned away, and you comfort me.
You are my salvation;
I will trust, and not be afraid:
for you are my strength and my song;
therefore with joy shall I draw water
from the wells of salvation.

Isaiah 12.1–3*

Blessed be God,
the Father of our Lord Jesus Christ,
the Father of mercies,
and the God of all comfort.

2 Corinthians 1.3

GOD IS MY SHEPHERD

God is my shepherd; there is nothing I need.
God lets me lie down in green pasture,
and leads me to pools of still water.
God refreshes my spirit, and shows me the right path.

If I lost my footing in the shadows,
and fell into the darkest valley, I would remain fearless.
For you are with me, to guide, instruct and comfort me.

You prepare a rich feast in front of my enemies.
You anoint me with oil, and my cup runs over.
I know that your goodness and mercy are always with me;
and I will dwell in the peace of God's house for ever.

Psalm 23*

CHRIST, MY EXAMPLE

O Christ, you suffered on my behalf
and left me your example,
that I should follow in your steps.

O Christ, you are my example!

You committed no sin,
you were guilty of no falsehood.

O Christ, you are my example!

When you were abused
you did not retaliate.

O Christ, you are my example!

When you suffered,
you uttered no threats,
but delivered yourself up to him who judges justly.

O Christ, you are my example!

You carried my sins in your own person on the cross,
so that I might cease to live for sin
and begin to live for righteousness.

O Christ, you are my example!

I was straying like a sheep,
but now you have turned me towards you,
the Shepherd and Guardian of my soul.

O Christ, you are my example!

1 Peter 2.21–25*

To whom shall we go?

Lord, to whom shall we go?
You have the words of eternal life.
And we believe and are sure
that you are the Christ,
the Son of the living God.

John 6.68–69*

O Lord, you show mercy
to those who have no one else to turn to.

Hosea 14.3

THE WAY, TRUTH AND LIFE

Son of God,
you are the way,
we follow you.

You are the truth,
we trust in you.

You are the life,
we live for you.

John 14.6*

KNOWING GOD IS THERE

O Lord, you have searched me, and known me.
You know when I sit down and when I rise up,
you understand my thoughts from afar.
You encompass my path and my lying down,
and are acquainted with all my ways.
Not a word leaves my lips, O Lord,
without your knowing it completely.
You are behind me and before me,
you have laid your hand upon me.
Such knowledge is too wonderful for me;
it is high, too high for me to reach.
Where shall I go from your Spirit?
or where shall I flee from your presence?
If I ascend up into heaven, you are there;
if I make my bed under the earth, you are there.
If I take the wings of the morning,
and dwell in the uttermost parts of the sea,
even there your hand will lead me,
and your right hand will hold me.
If I say, 'Surely the darkness shall cover me,'
even the night shall be light about me.
The darkness cannot conceal you;
but the night shines as the day:
the darkness and the light are both alike to you.
How precious also are your thoughts to me, O God!
How great is the sum of them!
If I should count them,
they are more in number than the sand:
when I awake, I am still with you.

Psalm 139.1–12, 17–18*

LORD JESUS, WE HONOUR YOUR NAME

Lord Jesus,
though you were in the form of God,
you did not regard equality with God
as something to be exploited.

Lord Jesus, we honour your name.

And being found in human form,
you emptied yourself,
taking the form of a slave,
being born in human likeness.

Lord Jesus, we honour your name.

You humbled yourself
and became obedient to the point of death –
even death on a cross.

Lord Jesus, we honour your name.

Therefore God highly exalted you
and gave you the name that is above every name,
so that at your name every knee should bend,
in heaven and on earth and under the earth.

Lord Jesus, we honour your name.

And every tongue shall confess
that you are Lord,
to the glory of God the Father.

Lord Jesus, we honour your name.

Philippians 2.6–11*

A LIVING HOPE

Blessed be the God and Father
of our Lord Jesus Christ!
By his great mercy he has given us
a new birth into a living hope
through the resurrection of Jesus Christ
from the dead,
and into an inheritance that is imperishable,
undefiled, and unfading,
kept in heaven for all
who are being protected by the power of God
through faith for a salvation
ready to be revealed in the last time.

1 Peter 1.3–5*

A HEAVENLY KINGDOM

Grace and peace be yours from God,
who is, who was, and who is to come,
and from the seven spirits
in front of his throne,
and from Jesus Christ,
the faithful witness,
the first to be raised from death.
He loves us, and by his death
he has freed us from our sins
and made us a kingdom of priests
to serve his God and Father.
To Jesus Christ be the glory and power
for ever and ever!
Amen.

Revelation 1.4–6

The Lord will rescue me from all evil
and take me safely into his heavenly kingdom.
To him be glory for ever and ever!

2 Timothy 4.18

KING OF THE NATIONS

Lord, there is no one like you;
you are mighty,
and your name is great and powerful.
Who would not honour you,
the king of all nations?
You deserve to be honoured.
There is no one like you.
You, Lord, are the true God,
you are the living God
and the eternal king.

Jeremiah 10.6–7, 10

How great and wonderful are all your works,
Lord God Almighty;
upright and true are all your ways, King of nations.
Who does not revere and glorify your name, O Lord?
For you alone are holy,
and all nations will come and adore you
for the many acts of saving justice you have shown.

Revelation 15.3–4

KING OF KINGS

To the eternal King,
the undying, invisible and only God,
be honour and glory for ever and ever;
who at the due time will be revealed by God,
the blessed and only Ruler of all,
the King of kings and the Lord of lords;
who alone is immortal,
whose home is in inaccessible light;
whom no human being has seen or is able to see:
to him be honour and everlasting power.
Amen.

1 Timothy 1.17; 6.15–16*

To God be the glory

O the depth of the riches and wisdom
and knowledge of God!
How unsearchable are his judgements
and how inscrutable his ways!
'For who has known the mind of the Lord?
Or who has been his counsellor?'
'Or who has given a gift to him,
to receive a gift in return?'
For from him and through him
and to him are all things.
To him be the glory for ever.
Amen.

Romans 11.33–36

THE ONLY WISE GOD

To God who is able to strengthen us
according to the gospel of Jesus Christ,
according to the revelation of the mystery
that was kept secret for long ages
but is now disclosed,
and through the prophetic writings
is made known to all,
according to the command of the eternal God,
to bring about the obedience of faith –
to the only wise God,
through Jesus Christ,
be the glory for ever!
Amen.

Romans 16.25–27*

Now to him who is able to keep us from falling,
and to present us faultless
before the presence of his glory
with eternal joy,
to the only wise God our Saviour,
be glory and majesty, dominion and power,
both now and ever.
Amen.

Jude 24–25*

ARROW PRAYERS

You are my lamp, O Lord.
You lighten my darkness.

2 Samuel 22.29*

O Lord God of heaven, the great and terrible God,
you keep covenant and mercy for them that love you
and observe your commandments.

Nehemiah 1.5*

The Lord gave, and the Lord has taken away;
blessed be the name of the Lord.

Job 1.21*

Remember, O God,
my life is only a breath.

Job 7.7

Deliverance belongs to the Lord!

Jonah 2.9

My soul magnifies the Lord,
and my spirit rejoices in God my Saviour.

Luke 1.46–47*

Lord, remember me when you come into your kingdom.

Luke 23.42*

Father, into your hands I commend my spirit.

Luke 23.46*

Lord, I believe.

John 9.28

My Lord and my God.

John 20.28

Lord; you know that I love you.

John 21.16

Lord, you are God,
you have made heaven and earth,
and the sea, and all that is in them!

Acts 4.24*

Lord Jesus, receive my spirit.

Acts 7.59

O God and Father of all,
you are above all, and through all, and in us all.

Ephesians 4.6*

PART 2

CONFESSION

SEEKING GOD'S FORGIVENESS

FORGIVE MY HIDDEN FAULTS

The law of the Lord is perfect,
reviving the soul.
The statutes of the Lord are trustworthy,
making wise the simple.
The precepts of the Lord are right,
giving joy to the heart.
The commands of the Lord are radiant,
giving light to the eyes.
The fear of the Lord is pure,
enduring for ever.
The ordinances of the Lord are sure
and altogether righteous.
They are more precious than gold,
than much pure gold;
they are sweeter than honey,
than honey from the comb.
By them is your servant warned;
in keeping them there is great reward.
Who can discern his errors?
Forgive my hidden faults.
Keep your servant also from wilful sins;
may they not rule over me.
Then will I be blameless,
innocent of great transgression.
May the words of my mouth
and the meditation of my heart
be pleasing in your sight,
O Lord, my Rock and my Redeemer.

Psalm 19.7–14

Forgive all my sins

Make me to know your ways,
O Lord; teach me your paths.
Lead me in your truth, and teach me,
for you are the God of my salvation;
for you I wait all day long.
Be mindful of your mercy, O Lord,
and of your steadfast love,
for they have been from of old.
Do not remember the sins of my youth
or my transgressions;
according to your steadfast love remember me,
for your goodness' sake, O Lord!

My eyes are ever towards the Lord,
for he will pluck my feet out of the net.
Turn to me and be gracious to me,
for I am lonely and afflicted.
Relieve the troubles of my heart,
and bring me out of my distress.
Consider my affliction and my trouble,
and forgive all my sins.

Psalm 25.4–7, 15–18

GOD KNOWS

Lord God,
hear from heaven your dwelling place,
and forgive.
Give to everyone according to their ways.
For you alone know the thoughts
of the human heart.

1 Kings 8.39*

Almighty Lord,
you are a just judge;
you test people's thoughts and feelings.
I have placed my cause in your hands.

Jeremiah 11.20

THE WEIGHT OF SIN

O my God, I am too ashamed
to lift up my face to you, my God,
because our sins are higher than our heads
and our guilt has reached to the heavens.
Here we are before you in our guilt,
though because of it not one of us
can stand in your presence.

Ezra 9.6, 15

Our transgressions and our sins
weigh upon us,
and we waste away because of them;
how then can we live?

Ezekiel 33.10

MAKE ME CLEAN

Be merciful to me, O God,
because of your constant love.
Because of your great mercy
wipe away my sins!
Wash away all my evil
and make me clean from my sin!

I recognize my faults;
I am always conscious of my sins.
I have sinned against you – only against you –
and done what you consider evil.
So you are right in judging me;
you are justified in condemning me.
I have been evil from the time I was born;
from the day of my birth I have been sinful.

Sincerity and truth are what you require;
fill my mind with your wisdom.
Remove my sins, and I will be clean;
wash me and I will be whiter than snow.
Let me hear the sounds of joy and gladness;
and though you have crushed me and broken me,
I will be happy once again.
Close your eyes to my sins
and wipe out all my evil.

Create a pure heart in me, O God,
and put a new and loyal spirit in me.
Do not banish me from your presence;
do not take your holy spirit away from me.
Give me again the joy that comes from your salvation,
and make me willing to obey you.

Psalm 51.1–12

My mind was embittered

My feet had almost slipped,
my foothold had all but given way,
because boasters roused my envy
when I saw how the wicked prosper.
No painful suffering for them!
They are sleek and sound in body;
they are not in trouble like ordinary mortals,
nor are they afflicted like other folk.
Therefore they wear pride like a necklace
and violence like a robe that wraps them round.
Their eyes gleam through folds of fat,
while vain fancies flit through their minds.
Their talk is all mockery and malice;
high-handedly they threaten oppression.

My mind was embittered,
and I was pierced to the heart.
I was too brutish to understand,
in your sight, God, no better than a beast.
Yet I am always with you;
you hold my right hand,
you guide me by your counsel
and afterwards you will receive me with glory.
Whom have I in heaven but you?
And having you, I desire nothing else on earth.
Though heart and body fail,
yet God is the rock of my heart,
my portion for ever.

Psalm 73.2–8, 21–26

FROM THE DEPTHS

From the depths of my despair
I call to you, Lord.
Hear my cry, O Lord;
listen to my call for help!
If you kept a record of our sins,
who could escape being condemned?
But you forgive us,
so that we should stand in awe of you.

Psalm 130.1–4

Lord, because of you my soul will live.
Give my spirit rest;
restore me and give me life.
Bitterness, not prosperity, had been my lot,
but your love saved me from the pit of destruction;
for you have thrust all my sins behind you.

Isaiah 38.16–17

A CONTRITE SPIRIT

High and holy God,
who inhabits eternity,
who dwells in the high and holy place,
and also with those who are contrite
and humble in spirit:
you restore the spirit of the humble,
and revive the heart of the contrite.
Do not continually accuse,
nor always be angry;
for then our spirits would grow faint before you,
even the souls that you have made.
Because of our greed you were angry.
You hid and were angry;
but we kept turning back to our own ways.
Now, we pray that you will heal us;
that you will lead and comfort those who mourn.
Give peace:
peace, to the far and the near, O Lord;
and heal us.

Isaiah 57.15–19*

LORD, LOOK UPON US, AND FORGIVE

Lord, look down from heaven
and see from your lofty throne, holy and glorious.
Where is your zeal and your might?
Your tenderness and compassion are withheld from us.

Lord, look upon us, and forgive.

But you are our Father,
our Redeemer from of old is your name.
Why, O Lord, do you make us wander from your ways
and harden our hearts so that we do not revere you?

Lord, look upon us, and forgive.

All of us have become like one who is unclean,
and all our righteous acts are like filthy rags;
we all shrivel up like a leaf,
and like the wind our sins sweep us away.

Lord, look upon us, and forgive.

No-one calls on your name
or strives to lay hold of you;
for you have hidden your face from us
and made us waste away because of our sins.

Lord, look upon us, and forgive.

Do not be angry beyond measure, O Lord;
do not remember our sins for ever.
Look upon us, we pray, for we are all your people.

Lord, look upon us, and forgive.

Isaiah 63.15–17; 64.6–9*

Do not abandon us

Even though our sins accuse us,
help us, Lord, as you have promised.
We have turned away from you many times;
we have sinned against you.
Why are you like a stranger,
like a traveller who stays for only one night?
Why are you like someone taken by surprise,
like a soldier powerless to help?
Surely, Lord, you are with us!
We are your people;
do not abandon us.

Jeremiah 14.7–9

Call us back to you, Lord.
Do not abandon us.
In your deep compassion, bring us back.
Do not hide your face in anger,
but in your everlasting kindness
have compassion on us.

Isaiah 54.6–8*

Do not give me up

Lord of compassion,
from my childhood you have loved me.
Like a mother you called me,
but the more you called to me,
the more I went from you;
yet it was you who taught me to walk,
you took me up in your arms;
but I did not know that you healed me.
You led me with cords of human kindness,
with bands of love.
You bent down to me and fed me.
Lord of compassion,
do not give me up;
for you are God and no mortal,
the Holy One in our midst.

Hosea 11.1–4, 8–9*

HAVE COMPASSION

O God, there is no other god like you,
who pardons sin and transgression.
You do not stay angry for ever,
but delight to show mercy.
Have compassion on us;
tread our sins underfoot
and hurl them into the depths of the sea!

Micah 7.18–19*

Lord god, we have sinned

We have sinned,
we have done wrong,
we have acted wickedly,
we have betrayed your commandments and rulings
and turned away from them.

Lord God, we have sinned.

It is for the Lord our God to have mercy and to pardon,
since we have betrayed him,
and have not listened to the voice of our God
nor followed the laws he has given us.

Lord God, we have sinned.

Listen, my God, listen to us;
open your eyes and look at our plight.
Relying not on our upright deeds but on your great
    mercy,
we pour out our plea to you.

Lord God, we have sinned.

Listen, Lord!
Forgive, Lord!
Hear, Lord, and act!

Lord God, we have sinned.

Daniel 9.4–13, 18–19*

WHO WILL RESCUE ME?

I am a creature of flesh and blood,
sold as a slave to sin.
I do not understand my own behaviour;
I do not act as I mean to,
but I do things that I hate.
While I am acting as I do not want to,
I still acknowledge the Law as good,
so it is not myself acting,
but the sin which lives in me.
I know of nothing good living in me –
in my natural self, that is –
for though the will to do what is good is in me,
the power to do it is not:
the good thing I want to do,
I never do;
the evil thing which I do not want –
that is what I do.
What a wretched creature I am!
Who will rescue me
from this body doomed to death?
God – thanks be to you –
through Jesus Christ my Lord.

Romans 7.14–19, 24–25*

ARROW PRAYERS

Lord, I am not worth all the kindness
and faithfulness that you have shown me.

Genesis 32.10

We have sinned.

Judges 10.15

I have committed a grave sin.
I beg you to forgive your servant for this fault,
for I have acted very foolishly.

2 Samuel 24.10*

I spoke foolishly, Lord.

Job 40.3

I despise myself,
and repent in dust and ashes.

Job 42.6

Bring me back, let me come back,
for you are the Lord my God.

Jeremiah 31.18

Look, O Lord, at my agony,
at the anguish of my soul!
My heart is broken in sorrow for my sins.

Lamentations 1.20

Have pity on your people, Lord.

Joel 2.17

Sovereign Lord, forgive your people!

Amos 7.2

In wrath may you remember mercy.

Habakkuk 3.2

Jesus, have pity on me.

Mark 10.47

Father, I have sinned against heaven,
and before you.

Luke 15.18

God be merciful to me a sinner.

Luke 18.13

PART 3

THANKSGIVING

PRAISING GOD'S GREATNESS

God's Greatness

O Lord, our Lord,
your greatness is seen in all the world!

Your praise reaches up to the heavens;
it is sung by children and babies.
You are safe and secure from all your enemies;
you stop anyone who opposes you.

When I look at the sky, which you have made,
at the moon and the stars, which you set in their places –
what is man, that you think of him;
mere man, that you care for him?

Yet you made him inferior only to yourself;
you crowned him with glory and honour.
You appointed him ruler over everything you made;
you placed him over all creation:
sheep and cattle, and the wild animals too;
the birds and the fish
and the creatures in the seas.

O Lord, our Lord,
your greatness is seen in all the world!

Psalm 8

Surrounded with joy

Sing praise to the Lord,
all his faithful people!
Remember what the Holy One has done,
and give him thanks!
His anger lasts only a moment,
his goodness for a lifetime.
Tears may flow in the night,
but joy comes in the morning.

I felt secure and said to myself,
'I will never be defeated.'
You were good to me, Lord;
you protected me like a mountain fortress.
But then you hid yourself from me,
and I was afraid.

I called to you, Lord;
I begged for your help;
'What will you gain from my death?
What profit from my going to the grave?
Are dead people able to praise you?
Can they proclaim your unfailing goodness?
Hear me, Lord, and be merciful!
Help me, Lord!'

You have changed my sadness into a joyful dance;
you have taken away my sorrow
and surrounded me with joy.
So I will not be silent;
I will sing praise to you.
Lord, you are my God,
I will give you thanks for ever.

Psalm 30.4–12

MY HEART EXULTS

My heart exults in the Lord,
in the Lord I hold my head high;
I gloat over my enemies;
I rejoice because you have saved me.
There is none but you,
none so holy as the Lord,
none so righteous as our God.

Cease your proud boasting,
let no word of arrogance pass your lips,
for the Lord is a God who knows;
he governs what mortals do.
Strong men stand in mute dismay,
but those who faltered put on new strength.

The Lord metes out both death and life:
he sends down to the grave,
he can bring the dead up again.
Poverty and riches both come from the Lord:
he brings low and he raises up.
He lifts the weak out of the dust
and raises the poor from the refuse heap
to give them a place among the great,
to assign them seats of honour.

The foundations of the earth are the Lord's,
and he has set the world upon them.
He will guard the footsteps of his loyal servants
while the wicked will be silenced in darkness:
for it is not by strength that a mortal prevails.

1 Samuel 2.1–9*

Everything is yours

Yours, Lord, is the greatness,
the power, the glory,
the victory, and the majesty:
for all that is in heaven and earth is yours;
yours is the kingdom,
and you are exalted above all.
Both riches and honour come from you,
and you reign over all.
In your hand is power and might;
you inspire greatness, and give strength to all.

Now, our God, we thank you,
and praise your glorious name.
But who are we
that we should offer you anything?
For all things come from you,
and of your own have we given you.
We are strangers before you, and exiles,
as were all our ancestors:
our days on the earth are as a shadow,
and all we do is transient.
O Lord our God,
all this comes from you,
and everything is yours.

1 Chronicles 29.10–16*

A REFUGE FOR THE WEAK

God, I shall praise you to the heights,
I shall praise your name;
for you have accomplished marvels,
plans long-conceived, faithfully, firmly.
May mighty peoples honour you,
the city of pitiless nations hold you in awe;
for you are a refuge for the weak,
a refuge for the needy in distress,
a shelter from the storm, shade from the heat;
for the breath of the pitiless is like a winter storm.
Like heat in a dry land you calm the foreigners' tumult;
as heat under the shadow of a cloud,
so the song of the pitiless dies away.

Isaiah 25.1, 3–5*

KING FOR EVER

I will proclaim your greatness,
my God and king;
I will thank you for ever and ever.
Every day I will thank you;
I will praise you for ever and ever.
The Lord is great and is to be highly praised;
his greatness is beyond understanding.
The Lord is loving and merciful,
slow to become angry and full of constant love.
He is good to everyone
and has compassion on all he made.

All your creatures, Lord, will praise you,
and all your people will give you thanks.
They will speak of the glory of your
    royal power
and tell of your might,
so that everyone will know your mighty deeds
and the glorious majesty of your kingdom.
Your rule is eternal,
and you are king for ever.

Psalm 145.1–3, 8–13

Thanks be to god our redeemer

He grew up before God as a tender plant,
piercing through the parched earth.

Thanks be to God our Redeemer.

He has no imposing form or alluring beauty.
Despised, rejected,
a man of sorrows and a friend of grief:
we hid our faces from him.

Thanks be to God our Redeemer.

Surely he bore our sufferings,
carried our sorrows.
Yet we counted him an outcast:
struck down, condemned by God.

Thanks be to God our Redeemer.

But he was wounded for our wrongdoing,
bruised for our barbarity.
The chastisement he endured makes us whole;
and through his sufferings we are healed.

Thanks be to God our Redeemer.

We had wandered from the way like sheep,
each of us following our own path;
and God laid on him the guilt of us all.

Thanks be to God our Redeemer.

Oppressed, afflicted,
he makes no protest.
Like a lamb for the slaughter,
like a sheep before the shearer,
he accepts his fate in silence.

Thanks be to God our Redeemer.

They led him to the place of execution,
and who among us gave it a thought?
Yet it was God's will to let him suffer,
to make his life a sacrifice for sin.

Thanks be to God our Redeemer.

Therefore he shall see his children;
he will live for ever in God's favour.

Thanks be to God our Redeemer.

Isaiah 53.2–10*

GLORY TO THE FATHER AND TO THE SON

Father, glorify your Son
so that the Son may glorify you.

Glory to the Father, and to the Son.

You have given him authority over all people,
to give eternal life to all whom you have given him.

Glory to the Father, and to the Son.

And this is eternal life, that we may know you,
the only true God, and Jesus Christ whom you have sent.

Glory to the Father, and to the Son.

He glorified you on earth
by finishing the work that you gave him to do.

Glory to the Father, and to the Son.

So now, Father, glorify him in your own presence
with the glory that he had in your presence before the
    world existed.

Glory to the Father, and to the Son.

He made your name known
to those whom you gave him from the world.

Glory to the Father, and to the Son.

We were yours, and you gave us to him,
and we have kept your word.

Glory to the Father, and to the Son.

The glory that you have given him he has given us,
so that we may be one, as you are one.

Glory to the Father, and to the Son.

He in us and you in him,
that we may become completely one.

Glory to the Father, and to the Son.

So that the world may know that you have sent him
and have loved us even as you have loved him.

Glory to the Father, and to the Son.

Father, we desire to see his glory,
which you have given him because you loved him
before the foundation of the world.

Glory to the Father, and to the Son.

John 17.1–6, 22–24*

Knowing the father and the son

We thank you, Father, Lord of heaven and earth,
for hiding your truth from the wise and the intelligent
and revealing it to infants;
yes, Father, for such was your gracious will.
We thank you for handing over all things to your Son,
and that no one knows the Son except the Father,
and no one knows the Father except the Son
and anyone to whom the Son chooses to reveal him.

Matthew 11.25–27*

LET US GIVE THANKS!

Let us give thanks to the God and Father
of our Lord Jesus Christ,
who has blessed us with all spiritual blessings
in heavenly places in Christ:

Let us give thanks!

He has chosen us in him
before the foundation of the world,
that we should be holy
and without blame before him in love:

Let us give thanks!

He has adopted us as his children through Jesus Christ,
and has offered us redemption through his blood,
the forgiveness of sins,
according to the riches of his grace.

Let us give thanks!

Ephesians 1.3–7*

WE THANK YOU, OUR GOD, FOR YOUR LOVE

You have chosen us from the beginning
to be saved by the Spirit, who makes us holy,
and by faith in the truth.

We thank you, our God, for your love.

You have called us to this,
to claim as our own
the glory of our Lord Jesus Christ.

We thank you, our God, for your love.

You have helped us stand firm,
to keep the traditions that we were taught.

We thank you, our God, for your love.

You have given us encouragement and hope,
to strengthen us in every good word and deed.

We thank you, our God, for your love.

2 Thessalonians 2.13–17*

Holy is the Lord

Holy, holy, holy
is the Lord God, the Almighty;
who was, and is and is to come.
You are worthy, our Lord and God,
to receive glory and honour and power,
for you made the whole universe;
by your will, when it did not exist,
it was created.

Revelation 4.8, 11

Holy, holy, holy,
is the Lord of hosts:
the whole earth is full of his glory.

Isaiah 6.3

WORTHY IS THE LAMB

Worthy is the Lamb that was sacrificed
to receive power, riches, wisdom,
strength, honour, glory and blessing.
To the One seated on the throne and to the Lamb,
be all praise, honour, glory and power,
for ever and ever.

Revelation 5.12–13

Amen! Praise, glory, wisdom,
thanksgiving, honour, power, and might
belong to our God for ever and ever! Amen!

Revelation 7.12

PRAISE GOD!

Praise God!
Salvation, glory, and power
belong to our God!
True and just are his judgements!

Praise our God,
all his servants and all people,
both great and small,
who have reverence for him!

Praise God!
For the Lord, our Almighty God, is King!
Let us rejoice and be glad;
let us praise his greatness!

Revelation 19.1–2, 5–7

Arrow Prayers

May the Most High God,
who made heaven and earth, be praised!

Genesis 14.19–20

How great you are, O Lord God!
There is none like you;
neither is there any God beside you.

2 Samuel 7.22*

Blessed be the Lord God of Israel,
who made heaven and earth!

2 Chronicles 2.12*

Praise the Lord, for he is good;
his mercy endures for ever!

2 Chronicles 5.13*

Praise the beauty of holiness.

2 Chronicles 20.12

Give thanks to the Lord of hosts,
for the Lord is good,
for his steadfast love endures for ever!

Jeremiah 33.11

Praise the glory of the Lord in heaven above!

Ezekiel 3.12

Blessed be the King that comes in the name of the Lord:
peace in heaven, and glory in the highest.

Luke 19.38

Father, I thank you that you have heard me.

John 11.41*

Father, glorify your name.

John 12.28

Thanks be to God!

Romans 6.17

May God, who rules over all,
be praised for ever!

Romans 9.5

Thanks be to God,
who gives us the victory
through our Lord Jesus Christ.

1 Corinthians 15.57*

Let us thank God for his priceless gift.

2 Corinthians 9.15

To God be the glory for ever and ever!

Galatians 1.5

Glory be to God our Father, for ever and ever.

Philippians 4.20

PART 4

PETITION

ASKING GOD'S HELP

A PRELUDE TO PRAYER

O Lord my God,
listen to the prayer of your servant;
hear my cry and grant the requests
I bring before you today.

1 Kings 8.28*

Holy Spirit,
help me, weak as I am;
I do not know how I ought to pray.

See into my heart,
and plead for me
in groans that words cannot express.

Romans 8.26–27*

Help me, O God, always to be joyful;
to pray constantly;
and for all things to give you thanks,
knowing that this is your will for me
in Christ Jesus.

1 Thessalonians 5.16–18*

When I am weak

I pray, O Lord,
that I will not fall into temptation:
for the spirit is willing,
but the flesh is weak.

Matthew 26.41*

Your grace, O Lord, is all I need:
for your strength is made perfect in weakness.

2 Corinthians 12.9*

GOD OUR HOPE

Lord, have mercy on us.
We have put our hope in you.
Protect us day by day
And save us in times of trouble.

Isaiah 33.2

Heal me, O Lord, and I shall be healed;
save me, and I shall be saved;
for you are my praise.

Jeremiah 17.14

May the God of hope
fill us with all joy and peace in our faith,
so that in the power of the Holy Spirit
we may be rich in hope.

Romans 15.13*

You have always been my God

My God, my God, why have you abandoned me?
I have cried desperately for help,
but still it does not come.
During the day I call to you, my God,
but you do not answer;
I call at night, but get no rest.

It was you who brought me safely through birth,
and when I was a baby, you kept me safe.
I have relied on you since the day I was born,
and you have always been my God.
Do not stay away from me!
Trouble is near, and there is no one to help.

Psalm 22.1–2, 9–11

TEACH ME YOUR LAWS

Teach me, Lord, the meaning of your laws,
and I will obey them at all times.
Explain your law to me, and I will obey it;
I will keep it with all my heart.
Keep me obedient to your commandments,
because in them I find happiness.
Give me the desire to obey your laws
rather than to get rich.
Keep me from paying attention to
   what is worthless;
be good to me as you have promised.
Enable me to speak the truth at all times,
because my hope is in your judgements.
I will always obey your law,
for ever and ever.
I will live in perfect freedom,
because I try to obey your teachings.

Psalm 119.33–37, 43–45

MAKE ME STRONG

Gracious God,
fill me with the knowledge of your will
in all spiritual wisdom and understanding,
so that I may lead a life worthy of you,
fully pleasing to you,
bearing fruit in every good work.

Make me strong with all the strength
that comes from your glorious power,
enduring everything with patience,
while joyfully giving thanks
that you have enabled me to share
in the inheritance of the saints in the light.

For you have rescued us all
from the power of darkness
and transferred us
into the kingdom of your beloved Son,
in whom we have redemption,
the forgiveness of sins.

Colossians 1.9–14*

Slow to speak

Father,
let me not be quick with my mouth
or hasty in my heart to utter anything before you.
For you are in heaven and I am on earth,
so I will let my words be few.

Ecclesiastes 5.2*

Father,
if I am angry, do not let it lead me into sin;
and let not the sunset find me nursing my resentment.
Let no offensive talk pass my lips,
only what is good and helpful to the occasion.
Let me have done with all spite and bad temper,
with rage, insults and slander,
and with evil talk of any kind.

Ephesians 4.26, 29–31*

Father, make me quick to listen,
slow to speak and slow to be angry.

James 1.19*

A LIVING SACRIFICE

Merciful God,
I present my body as a living sacrifice,
holy and acceptable to you.

Let me not be conformed to this world,
but let me be transformed by the renewing of my mind,
so that I may discern what is your will –
what is good and acceptable and perfect.

May my love be genuine;
may I hate what is evil,
and hold fast to what is good.
May I rejoice in hope,
be patient in suffering,
persevere in prayer.

Help me to bless those who persecute me;
rejoice with those who rejoice,
weep with those who weep.
Help me to live in harmony with everyone;
not to be haughty,
but to associate with the lowly.

Do not let me claim to be wiser than I am.
Do not let me repay anyone evil for evil,
but let me take thought for what is noble in the sight of all.
If it is possible, so far as it depends on me,
let me live peaceably with all.

Do not let me be overcome by evil,
but let me overcome evil with good.

Romans 12.1–3, 9–21*

GIVE ME LOVE

I could speak with the voice of an angel;
but if I do not speak in love
my speech is meaningless.

I could tell the future,
understand all mysteries,
know everything there is to know;
I could have such faith
that nothing would be impossible;
but if I do not live in love
my life is worthless.

I could give everything I have to the poor;
I could give my whole life;
but if I do not give in love
my gift is pointless.

Therefore in your love, O God,
teach me to be compassionate and kind;
not envious, boastful or conceited.
Let me never be rude or self-serving;
never let me be provoked,
but always think the best of others.

May I bear no grudges
and take no pleasure in evil,
but may I delight in goodness and truth.
For then I will bear any burden,
I will trust, I will hope;
I will keep faith when all others give up.

My love will never fail.
Great plans will come to nothing;
fine speeches will be silenced;
the deepest knowledge will be exhausted.
For I can only see so far;
I can only say so much;
and I can only know a fraction of the Truth.

Only in the light of your perfection, O God,
will I find wholeness.
When I was a child, I spoke as a child;
I understood as a child;
I thought as a child.
But when I grew up,
I left my childish ways behind.

Now, I look for you,
as if peering through a darkened window;
but one day I will see you face to face.
Now, my understanding is partial and fragmented;
but one day I will know you,
just as you know me.

And so, for now, give me faith, hope and love.
These are all I need;
but, above all, give me love.

1 Corinthians 13*

TRUE LOVE

O Lord my God,
you are the one Lord:
I love you with all my heart,
and with all my soul,
and with all my mind,
and with all my strength.
Let me show my love for you
by loving my neighbour
as I love myself.

Mark 12.29–31*

Merciful Father,
teach me how to love my enemies,
do good to those who hate me,
bless those who curse me,
and pray for those who mistreat me.
May I be ready to give to everyone who asks;
may I always do to others
as I would they should do to me.

Luke 6.27–31*

CHRIST WITHIN

Father, I bow my knees before you.
I ask you, from the riches of your glory,
to strengthen me by your Spirit in my inner self;
I pray that Christ may dwell in my heart by faith;
that, being rooted and grounded in love,
I may be able to comprehend with all your saints
the breadth, and length, and depth, and height
of Christ's love, which passes knowledge;
that I may be filled with all the fullness of God.
For you are able to do so much more
than I can ever ask or even think of,
according to the power that works in me.
To you, Father, be glory through Christ Jesus
in the church and throughout all ages,
world without end. Amen.

Ephesians 3.14–21*

Father, let me live for you, knowing that it is not I,
but Christ who lives in me;
and that the life I live now I live by the faith of your Son,
who loved me, and gave himself for me.

Galatians 2.20*

THE WISDOM OF THE SPIRIT

Father of glory,
God of our Lord Jesus Christ:
give us your Spirit and we will be wise;
reveal yourself to us
and we will know you;
open the eyes of our understanding
and we will be enlightened;
call us to you
and we will hope in the riches of your glory.

Ephesians 1.17–18*

THE HARVEST OF RIGHTEOUSNESS

I pray that my love may overflow
more and more with knowledge and full insight
to help me to determine what is best,
so that on the day of Christ
I may be pure and blameless,
having produced the harvest of righteousness
that comes through Jesus Christ
for the glory and praise of God.

Philippians 1.9–11*

Give me the wisdom from above,
pure, peaceable, gentle, willing to yield,
full of mercy and good fruits,
and without a trace of partiality or hypocrisy,
that I may reap a harvest of righteousness,
sown in peace for those who make peace.

James 3.17–18*

O GOD, MAKE US ONE

Clothe us, O God, with the new self,
and renew us in your image.
Make us one in Christ,
holy and beloved.

O God, make us one.

Clothe us with your compassion,
kindness, humility, meekness, and patience.
Help us to bear with one another:
to forgive each other,
just as you have forgiven us.

O God, make us one.

Above all, clothe us with love,
which binds everything together in perfect harmony.
And let the peace of Christ rule in our hearts,
to which we were called in the one body.
And let us be thankful.

O God, make us one.

Let the word of Christ dwell in us richly.
And whatever we do, in word or deed,
may we do it in the name of the Lord Jesus,
giving thanks to God the Father through him.

O God, make us one.

Colossians 3.10–17*

HELP US, LORD, AND SAVE US!

Since we are flesh and blood
you too shared our humanity.

Help us, Lord, and save us!

Through your death
you set us free from our fear of death.

Help us, Lord, and save us!

You became like us in every way,
in order to be our merciful and
faithful High Priest.

Help us, Lord, and save us!

Because you suffered when you were tempted,
you are able to help us when we are tempted.

Help us, Lord, and save us!

Hebrews 2.14–18*

A GOOD HEART

Oh that you would bless me,
and expand my heart;
that your hand might be with me,
and that you would keep me
from all evil and grief!

1 Chronicles 4.10*

My God, let me serve you
with a pure heart and a willing mind:
for you search all human hearts,
and understand all human thoughts.

1 Chronicles 28.9*

I ask you, O Lord, to remember
how I have walked before you in truth
and with a pure heart,
and have done what is right in your sight.

2 Kings 20.3*

A DESIRE TO DO GOOD

Father of compassion
God of all comfort,
who comforts me in all my troubles,
may I comfort those in any trouble
with the comfort I myself have received from you.
Just as the sufferings of Christ flow over into my life,
so also through Christ may my comfort overflow
into the lives of others.

2 Corinthians 1.3–5*

Gracious God,
I desire to use in service to others
the gift I have received from you.
Grant that I may give it
with the strength you give to me,
so that in all things glory may be given to·you
through Jesus Christ,
to whom belong glory and power
for ever and ever.
Amen.

1 Peter 4.10–11*

FOR THE GLORY OF GOD

May the God of perseverance and encouragement
give us all the same purpose,
so that with one heart we may give glory
to the God and Father of our Lord Jesus Christ.
May we accept one another for the sake of God's glory,
as Christ accepted us.

Romans 15.5–7*

We pray that God will make us worthy of our call,
and by his power fulfil all our desires for goodness,
and complete all that we do through faith;
so that the name of the Lord Jesus Christ
may be glorified in us, and us in him,
by the grace of our God and the Lord Jesus Christ.

2 Thessalonians 1.11–12*

Now may the God of peace,
who brought back from the dead our Lord Jesus,
the great shepherd of the sheep,
by the blood of the eternal covenant,
make us complete in everything good
so that we may do his will,
working among us that which is pleasing in his sight,
through Jesus Christ,
to whom be the glory for ever and ever.
Amen.

Hebrews 13.20–21*

THE PEACE OF GOD

Lord,
give me your peace,
the peace that transcends all understanding.
May it guard my heart and mind in Christ Jesus.
May it fill my thoughts with whatever is true,
whatever is right, pure, lovely, admirable,
excellent and worthy of praise.
Give me your peace, Lord,
and may it always
be with me.

Philippians 4.7–9*

May the God of peace
sanctify me through and through,
and may my whole being –
spirit, soul and body –
be kept blameless
at the coming of my Lord Jesus Christ.

1 Thessalonians 5.23*

May the Lord of peace
give us peace at all times and in every way.
The Lord be with us all.

2 Thessalonians 3.16*

GOD WITH US

May the Lord our God be with us;
may he never leave us, nor forsake us:
that he may draw us closer to him,
to walk in all his ways,
and to keep his commandments.

1 Kings 8.57–58*

May the grace of our Lord Jesus Christ,
the love of God,
and the fellowship of the Holy Spirit
be with us all.

2 Corinthians 13.14*

ARROW PRAYERS

O Lord God, I pray you, give me success this day.
Genesis 24.12*

Let me see the dazzling light of your presence.
Exodus 33.18

Almighty Lord, look at me, your servant!
See my trouble and remember me!
1 Samuel 1.11

Speak, Lord,
your servant is listening.
1 Samuel 3.9

God, make me strong!
Nehemiah 6.9

Remember me, O my God,
and spare me according to the greatness of your mercy.
Nehemiah 13.22*

I ask you, God, to let me have two things before I die:
keep me from lying, and let me be neither rich nor poor.
Proverbs 30.7

Do not let my mouth lead me into sin.
Ecclesiastes 5.6*

Lord, save me!
Matthew 14.30

I believe; help my unbelief!
Mark 9.24

Lord, teach us to pray.
Luke 11.1

Lord, increase our faith.
Luke 17.5

Jesus, Master, have mercy on us.
Luke 17.13

Not my will, but yours, be done.
Luke 22.42*

Stay with us;
the day is almost over and it is getting dark.
Luke 24.29

Lord, show us the Father; that is all we need.

John 14.8

What shall I do, Lord?

Acts 22.10

As opportunity offers, let us work for the good of all.

Galatians 6.10

May the Lord turn our hearts towards the love of God
and the perseverance of Christ.

2 Thessalonians 3.5*

O God, help us to grow in grace
and in the knowledge of our Lord and Saviour Jesus Christ.
To him be glory both now and for ever. Amen.

2 Peter 3.18*

Let us love, not in word or speech, but in truth and action.

1 John 3.18

O God, you are the true God.
Guard us against all false gods.

1 John 5.20–21*

PART 5

INTERCESSION

LOVING GOD'S WORLD

WE CRY, O LORD, FOR JUSTICE

Why, O Lord, do you stand far off?
Why do you hide yourself in times of trouble?
In his arrogance the wicked man hunts down the weak;
he boasts of the ravings of his heart.

We cry, O Lord, for justice.

He says to himself, 'Nothing will shake me;
I'll always be happy and never have trouble.'
His mouth is full of curses and lies and threats;
trouble and evil are under his tongue.

We cry, O Lord, for justice.

He lies in wait near the villages;
from ambush he murders the innocent,
watching in secret for his victims;
he catches the helpless and drags them off in his net.

We cry, O Lord, for justice.

His victims are crushed, they collapse;
they fall under his strength.
He says to himself, 'God has forgotten,
he covers his face and never sees.'

We cry, O Lord, for justice.

Arise, Lord! Lift up your hand, O God.
Do not forget the helpless.
Why does the wicked man revile God?
Why does he say to himself, 'He won't call me to account'?

We cry, O Lord, for justice.

The victim commits himself to you;
you are the helper of the fatherless.
Break the arm of the wicked and evil man;
call him to account for his wickedness.

We cry, O Lord, for justice.

You hear, O Lord, the desire of the afflicted;
you encourage them, and you listen to their cry,
defending the fatherless and the oppressed,
in order that man, who is from the earth,
may terrify no more.

We cry, O Lord, for justice.

Psalm 10*

Will you sweep away the righteous with the wicked?
Far be it from you to do such a thing!
Shall not the Judge of all the earth do what is just?

Genesis 18.23, 25

JUSTICE IS DRIVEN AWAY

Lord, our crimes against you are many.
Our sins accuse us.
We are well aware of them all.
We have rebelled against you, rejected you,
and refused to follow you.
We have oppressed others
and turned away from you.
Our thoughts are false;
our words are lies.
Justice is driven away,
and right cannot come near.
Truth stumbles in the public square,
and honesty finds no place there.
There is so little honesty
that anyone who stops doing evil
finds himself the victim of crime.

Isaiah 59.12–15

HOW LONG, O LORD?

How long, O Lord, must I call for help
but you do not listen?
Or cry out to you, 'Violence!'
but you do not save?
Why do you make me look at injustice?
Why do you tolerate wrong?
Destruction and violence are before me;
there is strife, and conflict abounds,
therefore the law is paralysed,
and justice never prevails.
The wicked hem in the righteous,
so that justice is perverted.
How long, O Lord, must I call for help
but you do not listen?

Habakkuk 1.2*

GOD OF ALL HUMANITY

God of all humanity,
to you we offer our petitions, prayers,
intercessions and thanksgivings for everyone:
for sovereigns and all in high office,
that all may lead tranquil and quiet lives,
free to practise their religion with dignity.
May our prayers be approved by God our Saviour,
whose will it is that all should find salvation
and come to know the truth.
For you are the only God,
and there is one mediator between God and humanity,
Christ Jesus, himself a man,
who sacrificed himself to win freedom for all,
revealing your purpose at your good time.

1 Timothy 2.1–6*

May the Lord increase and enrich our love
for each other and for all,
and may he so confirm our hearts in holiness
that we may be blameless in the sight of our God and Father
when our Lord Jesus comes with all his holy ones.

1 Thessalonians 3.12–13*

WONDERFUL COUNSELLOR

Wonderful Counsellor:
give the world the wisdom of your counsels.

Mighty God:
show the world the glory of your mightiness.

Everlasting Father:
hold the world in the arms of your unfailing love.

Prince of Peace:
unite the world in the service of your kingdom.

From now until the end of time.

Isaiah 9.6–7*

GOD WILL PARDON

We seek you and call upon you,
knowing you are near.
Let the wicked forsake their way,
and let the unrighteous change their thoughts:
let them return to the Lord,
and he will have mercy upon them;
let them turn to our God,
for he will abundantly pardon.
For your thoughts are not our thoughts,
neither are our ways your ways.
As the heavens are higher than the earth,
so are your ways higher than our ways,
and your thoughts than our thoughts.

Isaiah 55.5–9*

GOOD NEWS TO THE NEEDY

Lord God, anoint us with your Spirit,
that we may bring good news to the needy
and healing to the broken-hearted;
that we may proclaim liberty
to the captives of injustice and oppression,
and freedom to all who are trapped
in poverty and despair.

Isaiah 61.1*

You have shown us, O God, what is good;
and what you require of us.
So help us to act justly, and love mercy,
and walk humbly with our God.

Micah 6.8*

WHAT MATTERS MOST

Lord Jesus,
help us to let go of concerns about our lives,
what to eat, what to drink;
or about our bodies, what to wear.
Help us to see that life is more than food and drink,
and the body more than clothes.
Increase our faith in our heavenly Father,
who knows that we need all these things.
Increase our faith that our concern may be,
above everything else,
with the kingdom of God and his righteousness.

Matthew 6.25, 32–33*

WE LOOK FOR PEACE

We look for peace, but nothing good happens;
we hope for healing, but terror comes instead.
We have sinned against you, Lord;
we confess our own sins
and the sins of our ancestors.

Jeremiah 14.19–20

Merciful and tender God,
cause the bright dawn of salvation to rise on us,
to shine from heaven on all those
who live in the dark shadow of death,
and guide our steps into the paths of peace.

Luke 1.78–79

Lead us to the day

Teach us your ways, O Lord,
and we will walk in your paths.
Teach us to beat our swords into ploughs,
and our spears into pruning-knives.
Lead us to the day when nation shall not
rise up against nation,
neither shall they train for war any more.
Lead us to the day when everyone will live in peace
and nothing will make them afraid.

Micah 4.2–4*

No more tears

O Lord, we weep and lament,
but you can turn our sorrow into joy.
We are like a woman about to give birth.
Help us to see beyond the pangs
of this present sadness,
that we may forget the anguish,
and our hearts at last may rejoice.

John 16.20–22*

O God, we wait for the time
when you will live among us
and make your home among us;
when we will be your people,
and you will be our God: God with us.
You will wipe away all tears from our eyes;
there will be no more death,
and no more mourning or sadness or pain.
The world of the past will be gone.

Revelation 21.3–4*

THE LORD'S BANQUET

Prepare your banquet, Lord:
a banquet of rich food, a banquet of fine wines,
of succulent food, of well-strained wines.
Destroy the veil which used to veil all peoples,
the pall enveloping all nations;
destroy death for ever.
Wipe away the tears from every cheek;
take people's shame away everywhere on earth.
And on that day, we will say,
'Look, this is our God, in him we put our hope.
Let us exult and rejoice for he has saved us.'

Isaiah 25.6–9*

A NEW CREATION

We wait, O Lord, for what you have promised:
a new heaven and a new earth,
when the former things shall not be remembered or come
to mind;
when we shall be glad and rejoice for ever in what you
are creating;
when no more shall the sound of weeping be heard, or
the cry of distress;
when infants shall no longer live but a few days,
and old people shall live out a full lifetime;
when people shall build houses and inhabit them;
when they shall plant vineyards and eat their fruit;
when they shall not build and another inhabit;
when they shall not plant and another eat;
when they shall not labour in vain, or bear children for
calamity;
when the wolf and the lamb shall feed together,
and the lion shall eat straw like the ox;
but the serpent – its food shall be dust!
We wait, O Lord, for what you have promised.

Isaiah 65.17–25*

MAY ALL THE PEOPLES PRAISE YOU!

God, be merciful to us and bless us;
look on us with kindness,
so that the whole world may know your will;
so that all nations may know your salvation.

May the peoples praise you, O God;
may all the peoples praise you!

May the nations be glad and sing for joy,
because you judge the peoples with justice
and guide every nation on earth.

May the peoples praise you, O God;
may all the peoples praise you!

Psalm 67.1–5

The grace of God

The Lord bless you, and keep you:
the Lord make his face shine upon you,
and be gracious to you:
the Lord lift up his countenance upon you,
and give you peace.

Numbers 6.24–26*

May God our Father
and the Lord Jesus Christ
give you grace and peace.

Romans 1.7

May the God of all grace,
who called you to eternal glory in Christ,
restore, confirm, strengthen and support you.
His power lasts for ever and ever.
Amen.

1 Peter 5.10–11*

ARROW PRAYERS

May the nations administer true justice,
and show mercy and compassion to one another.

Zechariah 7.9*

Lord, save us: we perish.

Matthew 8.25

Lord Jesus, gather us to you,
as a hen gathers her chicks under her wings.

Matthew 23.37*

Glory to God in the highest,
and on earth peace, good will to all people.

Luke 2.14*

O God, stretch out your hand to heal
and perform miraculous signs and wonders
through the name of your holy servant Jesus.

Acts 4.30*

Our Lord, come!

1 Corinthians 16.22

May peace and mercy
be with all God's people!

Galatians 6.16

Almighty Lord, holy and true!
How long will it be until you judge the people on earth?

Revelation 6.10

So be it. Come, Lord Jesus!
May the grace of the Lord Jesus be with everyone.

Revelation 22.20–21

Arrow blessings

God be gracious to you.
Genesis 43.29*

The Lord be with you.
Ruth 2.4

The Lord bless you.
Ruth 2.4

May the Lord reward you for what you have done.
Ruth 2.12

The God of peace be with us all.
Romans 15.33*

The grace of our Lord Jesus Christ be with you.
1 Corinthians 16.23

May God the Father and the Lord Jesus Christ
give us peace and love with faith.
Ephesians 6.23*

May God's grace be with all who
love our Lord Jesus Christ in sincerity.

Ephesians 6.24*

Grace be with you.

Colossians 4.18

May grace and peace be yours.

1 Thessalonians 1.1

The Lord Jesus Christ be with your spirit.

2 Timothy 4.22

Grace be with us all.

Titus 3.15*

The grace of our Lord Jesus Christ be with your spirit.

Philemon 25

Peace to you all who are in Christ.

1 Peter 5.14

May grace and peace be yours in abundance
in the knowledge of God and of Jesus our Lord.

2 Peter 1.2

May God the Father and Jesus Christ, the Father's Son,
give us grace, mercy, and peace;
may they be ours in truth and love.

2 John 3

Peace be with you.

3 John 15

May mercy, peace, and love be yours in full measure.

Jude 2

PART 6

CONTEMPLATION*

LISTENING TO GOD'S WORDS

*For a brief explanation of this section,
see Introduction, page xvi.

I am who I am.

Exodus 3.14

I am the first, the last, the only God.

Isaiah 44.6

I am the Lord, the Creator of all things.

Isaiah 44.24

I am the high and holy God, who lives for ever.

Isaiah 57.15

I am merciful.

Jeremiah 3.12

I am everywhere in heaven and on earth.

Jeremiah 23.24

I am the Lord, and I do not change.

Malachi 3.6

I am the Lord your God.

Exodus 20.2

I am the Lord and I make you holy.

Leviticus 22.32

I am the God who forgives your sins.

Isaiah 43.25

I am the Lord who created you.

Isaiah 44.2

I am the one who saves you.

Isaiah 44.22

I am the one who strengthens you.

Isaiah 51.12

I am your Father.

Malachi 1.6

Worship no god but me.

Exodus 20.3

Do not abandon me.

Leviticus 19.4

Quietly trust in me.

Isaiah 30.15

Be silent and listen to me.

Isaiah 41.1

You are precious to me.

Isaiah 43.4

You belong to me.

Jeremiah 3.14

Seek me with all your heart.

Jeremiah 29.13

My spirit is like a fire.

Isaiah 33.11

My victory will endure for all time.

Isaiah 51.8

My love for you will never end.

Isaiah 54.10

My thoughts are not like yours.

Isaiah 55.8

My presence will protect you on every side.

Isaiah 58.8

My glory will shine on you.

Isaiah 60.19

My saving power will rise on you like the sun.

Malachi 4.2

I have heard your prayer.

Isaiah 38.5

I have called you by name – you are mine.

Isaiah 43.1

I have swept away your sins like a cloud.

Isaiah 44.22

I have written your name on the palms of my hands.

Isaiah 49.16

I have given you my power and my teachings.

Isaiah 59.21

I, the Lord, have saved you.

Isaiah 60.16

I have always loved you.

Malachi 1.2

You are stained red with sin,
but I will wash you clean as snow.

Isaiah 1.18

Do not be afraid; I will save you.

Isaiah 43.1

When you pass through deep waters,
I will be with you.

Isaiah 43.2

Even if a mother should forget her child,
I will never forget you.

Isaiah 49.15

With deep love, I will take you back.

Isaiah 54.7

I turned away angry for only a moment,
but I will show my love for ever.

Isaiah 54.8

When you pray, I will answer you.

Isaiah 58.9

I will not hold your sins against you.
Isaiah 43.25

I will give you the strength you need.
Isaiah 45.5

I will comfort you as a mother comforts her child.
Isaiah 66.13

I will not be angry with you for ever.
Jeremiah 3.12

I will not let you go unpunished.
Jeremiah 30.11

I will sprinkle clean water on you and make you clean.
Ezekiel 36.25

I will give you a new heart and a new mind.
Ezekiel 36.26

I will put my spirit in you.

Ezekiel 36.27

I will save you from everything that defiles you.

Ezekiel 36.29

I will be true and faithful.

Hosea 2.19

I will show you constant love and mercy.

Hosea 2.19

I will make you mine for ever.

Hosea 2.19

I will be with you – that is my promise.

Haggai 1.13

I will bless you.

Haggai 2.19

Ask, and you will receive.

Matthew 7.7

Seek, and you will find.

Matthew 7.7

Knock, and the door will be opened to you.

Matthew 7.7

Do you believe that I can heal you?

Matthew 9.28

Come to me, and I will give you rest.

Matthew 11.28

Learn from me, and you will find rest.

Matthew 11.29

I will be with you always.

Matthew 28.20

Follow me.

Mark 2.14

I have chosen you to be with me.

Mark 3.14

Be still!

Mark 4.39

Be healed of your trouble.

Mark 5.34

Don't be afraid, only believe.

Mark 5.36

What do you want me to do for you?

Mark 10.51

Have faith in God.

Mark 11.22

Be clean!

Luke 5.13

Your sins are forgiven.

Luke 5.20

Your faith has saved you.

Luke 7.50

Where is your faith?

Luke 8.25

Your Father is pleased to give you the Kingdom.

Luke 12.32

God knows your heart.

Luke 16.15

Peace be with you.

Luke 24.36

I am the bread of life.

John 6.35

I am the light of the world.

John 8.12

I am the gate for the sheep.

John 10.7

I am the good shepherd.

John 10.11

I am the resurrection and the life.

John 11.25

I am the way, the truth, and the life.

John 14.6

I am the real vine.

John 15.1

Because I live, you also will live.

John 14.19

You are in me, just as I am in you.

John 14.20

Remain united to me, and I will remain united to you.

John 15.4

I love you just as the Father loves me.

John 15.9

You will have peace by being united to me.

John 16.33

Stop your doubting, and believe!

John 20.27

Do you love me?

John 21.16

Acknowledgements

The following Scripture quotations are taken from the Good News Bible © 1994 published by the Bible Societies/Harper-Collins Publishers Ltd, UK Good News Bible © American Bible Society 1966, 1971, 1976, 1992. Used with permission.

Genesis 14.19–20; 32.10; Exodus 3.14; 20.2; 20.3; 33.18; Leviticus 19.4; 22.32; Ruth 2.12; 1 Samuel 1.11; 3.9; Nehemiah 6.9; Job 7.7; 13.22–28; 14.1–2, 7–12, 14–17; 40.3; Psalms 8; 16.5–11; 22.1–2, 9–11; 30.4–12; 42.1–3, 5; 51.1, 2, 10; 51.1–12; 67.1–5; 119.33–37, 43–45; 130.1–4; 131.1–2; 135.3; 136.1; 145.1–3, 8–13; Proverbs 30.7; Isaiah 1.18; 26.3, 8; 30.15; 33.2; 33.11; 38.5; 41.1; 43.1; 43.2; 43.4; 43.25; 44.2; 44.6; 44.22; 44.24; 45.5; 49.15; 49.16; 51.8; 51.12; 54.7; 54.8; 54.10; 55.8; 57.15; 58.8; 58.9; 59.12–15; 59.21; 60.16; 60.19; 66.13; Jeremiah 3.12; 3.14; 10.6–7, 10; 11.20; 14.7–9; 14.19–20; 16.19; 23.24; 29.13; 30.11; Lamentations 1.20; Ezekiel 3.12; 36.25; 36.26; 36.27; 36.29; Hosea 2.19; 14.3; Joel 2.17; Amos 7.2; Haggai 1.13; 2.19; Malachi 1.2; 1.6; 3.6; 4.2; Matthew 6.9–13; 7.7; 9.28; 11.28; 11.29; 27.46; 28.20; Mark 2.14; 3.14; 4.39; 5.34; 5.36; 10.51; 11.22; 14.36; Luke 1.78–79; 4.8; 5.13; 5.20; 7.50; 8.25; 12.32; 16.15; 24.29; 24.36; John 6.35; 8.12; 10.7; 10.11; 11.25; 14.6; 14.8; 14.19; 14.20; 15.1; 15.4; 15.9; 16.33; 20.27; 21.16; Acts 22.10; Romans 1.7; 6.17; 9.5; 2 Corinthians 1.3; 9.15; Galatians 1.5; 6.16; Ephesians 1.3, 6; Philippians 4.6; Colossians 1.3; 1 Thessalonians 1.1; 2 Timothy 4.18; 1 John 1.8–9; 3.18; 3.21, 22; 4.16–18; 5.14; 2 John 3; Jude 2; Revelation 1.4–6; 6.10; 7.12; 19.1–2, 5–7; 22.20–21.

Index to Prayers

Index of Themes

CRLO JE

140